To Carole!

Manifest Your Year

Exercises to Make Your Wishes Come True

Manifest your best life!

Melanie Barnum (Bethel, CT) is a psychic, medium, intuitive counselor, life coach, and hypnotist who has been practicing professionally for more than twe3nty years. She was a VIP Reader at Psychic Out, a gathering of the nation's foremost psychics, organized by Court TV. Barnum regularly sees clients in her Ridgefield, CT, office and over the phone and internet and is a member of the National Guild of Hypnotists (NGH) and the International Association of Counselors and Therapists (IACT).
www.MelanieBarnum.com

Manifest Your Year

Exercises to Make Your Wishes Come True

MELANIE BARNUM

ISBN-13: 978-0-9988345-1-1

Author's Note

The Author of this book is not in any way diagnosing or offering any medical advice or suggesting the information contained herein should be used in replace of or instead of any professional counseling or professional medical treatment, therapy or prescriptions. This book should in no way be used as an alternative to any type of mental or physical professional help.

The Author of this book shall be held harmless from any injuries arising from following any exercises in any part of this book. It is strongly suggested you contact your physician or therapist if you experience any mental or physical symptoms. Melanie Barnum is not a doctor and does not claim to be and this book should not be used to treat any ailments you may have.

DEDICATION

I dedicate this book to everyone who reads it, who is brave enough to take the initiative to change their own lives and to bring about what they desire.

ACKNOWLEDGEMENT

I want to recognize and acknowledge everyone who has been a part of my life to this point. I appreciate how much you've all contributed to my learning process and my intuitive awareness. To all of my clients and my friends and family who continue to believe in my gifts and my ability to help others,

THANK YOU!

CONTENTS

INTRODUCTION

I want you to have it all! It is time for you to step into your power and find your joy! I've worked with clients from all around the world and have assembled the 52 most discussed and most asked for manifestation topics in a simple, easy to use guide just for you.

Manifesting does not have to be difficult or complicated. Rather, it centers around your intention, so each exercise is designed to draw forth the intended outcome. Remember, it is entirely up to you which you choose to initiate and use to make changes, personally, in your life. Enjoy them!

The exercises on the following pages were created for you, by me. I've tuned into my intuition for each specific manifestation instruction and shared them here with you. You might find them interesting and some may resonate with you more than others. Some may seem silly, even, and simple. They are designed that way, intentionally.

So often we get hung up on the belief that in order to bring about change we have to work really hard. We think we have to be very serious and disregard anything or anyone that may bring fun into the equation, because, after all, how can having fun create what we want? It would be too easy, right? Wrong!

When I set out to write this book I tuned into my intuition and allowed that I would honor what came through, regardless of how silly or seemingly inconsequential it may appear. The result was 52 exercises filled with surprisingly different methods to manifest a wide variety of circumstances and belongings.

The universe is vast and filled with abundance, just waiting to be tapped into. It's time for you to access this abundance. Your focus, through these manifestation exercises, will help provide the structure you've been missing to draw the energy to you, which will allow the universe to accommodate you and your wishes.

You attract what you send out. Simply explained this means your attitude as you go through life will come back to you ten-fold. Coming from a place of gratitude and fulfillment rather than fear and lack will instantly change the energy you'll experience. You will find yourself welcoming in more positivity and a flow of abundance in all areas.

For example, I had my client try something last week. I told her to tell herself a story that she didn't believe, about who she was, and she told me about her results the other day.

"For the past three days I have decided to only be positive--I tell myself I am incredible, I am beautiful, and I have amazing friends. And, I can tell you that over the last three days I have been so happy!"

This was not coming from a place of ego, rather this was the opposite of her ego. This was coming from a dip in her self-esteem. She was coming out of a tough patch in a relationship and she needed a boost. This was a perfect time to try this experiment and it changed her life! Being positive had attracted and actually created and manifested positive energy all around her.

Manifesting is not about ego. It's not about bragging rights, either. It's about creating a life you want to live. You don't need anyone to tell you what you want. Everyone is different and is going through a different stage in life. However, we can all use some help bringing about change. What better way to attract abundance than to manifest? It is through positive change that we can make a difference in our own lives as well as the lives of others, so why not start living our best lives now?

Why This Book?

What do you want? What do you need? This book can help you! That, my friends, is the million-dollar question. If we can determine what we need to manifest to live our greatest life, we can accomplish our most sought after and most elusive goal-the pursuit of happiness. Our objective is not to merely make it through, one day at a time, as we may have been doing. Rather, it is to enjoy it, living on purpose, feeling joy and spreading kindness because we are truly content.

This 52-week guide can be used once a week to help you manifest your greatest wishes, hopes and desires. Alternatively, you may find you'd rather jump around, moving to the week that resonates with you in that moment or that you may find necessary at the time. For example, if you find yourself looking for a new job, you might choose to jump ahead to ***Week 45-New Job***. You could make it more successful by combining it with ***Week 13-Success in your Career*** and ***Week 9-Love Your Career.*** You can utilize this guide in any order that works for you.

How to Manifest

Manifesting is the act of creating that which you desire. It is about making what you wish a reality. In essence, manifesting is recognizing and bringing about what you want, without really working to make it happen. This does not mean that you don't put any effort into it, it just means you produce it in a different way. You create the energy around it by building the intention. You construct that which you desire by utilizing the energy that connects everything in the universe. And, then, you are able to manifest.

Believing it is possible to manifest what you want is key to actually manifesting what you want. Wanting something is only the first step. Believing that it can be is critical. Again, it's about sending the energy out into the universe. If you don't believe what you desire is achievable or even slightly viable there is no way it will come to fruition. Imagining you can manifest what you want will bring you that much closer to creating the life you'll love.

Being grateful will also help you manifest what you desire. After each manifestation exercise, you'll need to express gratitude. Say 'Thank You!' for the entire week. Say it out loud, to the world, for bringing that which you need, what you want, to you. This is an important part of the process. Expressing your appreciation is a necessary exchange of energy when manifesting anything.

Regardless of whether you choose to manifest weekly or jump around, you'll want to follow the instructions for each individual manifestation. Each exercise can be done once (unless directed otherwise) or can be repeated daily for the entire week. The exercises will be simple and easy to follow, generally allowing you to perform them almost like natural spells. There is also an element of self-hypnosis which gives you the option of going back and repeating the exercises over time to kind of re-charge your manifestation. Remember, it's about distilling and extracting the essence of what you want and setting your intention and then allowing the universe to do it's best to bring you what you desire, as long as it's for your greater good.

So, what are you waiting for? It's time to make your wishes come true. Get to manifesting!

MANIFESTATION EXERCISES

~Week 1~
Welcome
A Happy Year

◆◆◆

What You'll Need

Paper, pen, glitter

Preferable Location

Outside

Manifestation Exercise

Welcoming a new year, a positive and abundant new year, means opening your energy to what you want to manifest for the coming year. In order to do this, take a minute to sit down and think about what's really important to you. Think of what you want to bring into your life. Decide what is most important to you for the year to come.

Then, write down the top five things you wish to manifest. What are your wishes for the upcoming year? Write them each down on their own piece of paper. If you have a hard time narrowing it down, perhaps choosing one goal from each of the following categories will help: love, health, career, family and finances.

Once you've written them down, bring your list and your glitter outside. Pour a bit of glitter onto your first paper and say your manifestation wish out loud. Then, blow the glitter out into the air, sending your wish into the universe to be manifested for you!

Repeat until you are done with all five of your manifestation wishes. Repeat each up to 8 times, to increase your upcoming happiness for the upcoming year to infinity!

Say 'THANK YOU' to the universe for manifesting your Happy Year!

~Week 2~
Opening to A Healthy Lifestyle

◆◆◆

What You'll Need

Dirt/earth, seeds Spoon or spade

Preferable Location

Outside (if inside use potting soil in a pot)

Manifestation Exercise

What does a healthy lifestyle mean to you? A healthy lifestyle may seem like a huge generalization, but that's ok because you will have plenty of opportunity to manifest specifics in the coming weeks. For now, focus on the grand scheme of bringing in a healthy lifestyle overall.

Think about what that means to you. It could encompass many goals, such as a healthy weight and exercise regime. It may point to maintaining healthy relationships. It could represent living with low stress and might even suggest emotional freedom. Stability in your life may be the overall theme of opening to a healthy lifestyle. There's no right answer—this is personal to you.

When you're ready, take your seeds out and, using your spoon or spade, dig a small hole and plant them, one at a time, while repeating the words, 'I am manifesting a healthy lifestyle' over and over until you are done with your seeds. Then, cover them completely, stand up and spin around three times, repeating your manifestation with each turn. Thank the universe!

Now that you've planted your seeds, relax, and let your healthy lifestyle begin!

~Week 3~
Increase Your Self-Esteem

◆◆◆

What You'll Need

Pitcher or 2 bottles of water Large glass or cup

(which can be closed or sealed)

Preferable Location

Inside or Outside

Manifestation Exercise

Sometimes, manifesting something positive requires ridding ourselves of negativity first. Such is the case with this exercise. Take your glass and your water and think about anything that may be decreasing your self-esteem or anything that might be causing yourself-esteem to be naturally low. As you think of each issue, pour a bit of water into the glass, releasing that issue into the glass with the flow of the water. When you've exhausted every reason you can imagine that you feel your self-esteem isn't as high as you'd like it to be seal the cup tightly. Now, shake it up, saying the words, 'I release my negative self-esteem beliefs' aloud. Repeat until you are ready to stop, until you feel you are done and ready to move on, but at least 11 times. Then, repeating that same phrase, dump the water, either on the ground if outside, or down the toilet if inside.

Now, rinse the cup clean. With the fresh water, begin stating aloud positive affirmations while filling the cup. Say, 'I am more than enough', 'I am worthy', 'I am fantastic', 'I am beautiful', 'I am strong', 'I am smart', 'I am kind' and continue with any other affirmations that are personal or important to you until you've filled up your cup with positive self-esteem energy. When you are done, drink up! Fill your body with healing, powerful, fresh new confidence!

Thank the universe for increasing your ever-budding self-esteem!

~Week 4~
Establishing A Healthy Weight

◆◆◆

What You'll Need

An image of, or an actual analog scale (not digital)

Preferable Location

Inside

Manifestation Exercise

Establishing a healthy weight is not always about a number. But for this exercise we will utilize a number to help create an achievable interpretation of the goal you want to reach. Don't get hung up on the number, use it as a loose guide to manifesting your perfect, healthy weight!

Look at the image of the scale or the real scale. See the lines and the numbers. Imagine the weight you are now and then imagine the weight you wish to be, or somewhere close to where you think you'd like to aim for as your healthy weight. This is what you are going to manifest. Now, determine if you want to gain or lose weight during the coming year. Visualize where you are starting at, your beginning weight and close your eyes.

Next, imagine where you want to be. If you need to gain to achieve your healthy weight, imagine you are standing on the pivot point of the scale and begin rotating to the right, watching in your mind as the scale climbs until you reach your ideal weight. Once there, stop. See the scale as it reads between your feet as you look down, the perfect healthy weight for you.

Alternatively, if you desire to lose weight, using yourself as the pivot on the scale turn your body to the left, rotating while watching the numbers decrease until you see your healthy weight between your toes as you visualize your healthy weight. When you are done, step off the scale and open your eyes.

Now, say the words, 'I am easily at my healthy weight.' Repeat this 11 times, and every day for the following week. Thank the universe out loud for manifesting your perfect, healthy weight in the year to come!

~Week 5~
Welcoming Wealth

◆◆◆

What You'll Need

2 or more gold and silver candles Coins and jewelry

Preferable Location

Inside

Manifestation Exercise

Welcoming wealth is about being open to wealth and leaving poverty consciousness behind. Too often we get stuck in a rut, keeping ourselves energetically blocked from achieving any semblance of financial security. This manifestation exercise should be used to rid yourself of that and open yourself to moving forward with a clear belief and awareness of wealth consciousness instead!

Over the next week you will need to have access to your candles, which you will place in a prominent place in your living or working space. Whether it be in your living room, your office or even your kitchen, it should be somewhere you spend a lot of time. Place the candles together, on the same candle holder or plate, touching each other. Around the candles, place gold and silver coins, and jewelry that is either real or that represents real gold and silver.

Then, every evening light the candles, saying the words, 'I have outlived poverty consciousness' as you light each one. When you have finished, say it one last time, then blow them out and touch all of the coins and jewelry. Then, in the morning, light the candles, and as you light each one say, 'I am welcoming wealth everyday'. Once they are all lit, repeat it again, and blow them out, touching all of the coins and jewelry again. Repeat this every day for a week.

Be sure to extend your gratitude to the universe for manifesting a new, wealthy life!

~Week 6~
Creating Positive Change

◆◆◆

What You'll Need

Jar

Post It or sticky note papers

Marker that can write on glass

Preferable Location

Inside

Manifestation Exercise

Creating positive change has many connotations. Positive change can cover many aspects in your life, from health to love to career to finances to family and everything in between. There's no reason to not address all of them and do a blanket manifestation for positive change!

Take your sticky note papers and write down something you want to change on one of them. Next, draw a big plus sign, or positive sign (+) over the entire post it, covering the negative thing you wish to change. Fold it and seal it to itself. Continue doing that until you can no longer think of anything else in your life that you want to change from more negative to more positive. Then, draw positive symbols on a couple more blank sticky notes, folding them the same way, enhancing each sheet with positive energy.

Next, one by one, put all of the newly charged positively energized notes into the jar while saying, 'I am creating positive change in my life, constantly' as you do. Continue until you have filled up the jar, going back and writing more if necessary.

Then, with your marker, draw the positive signs all over the outside of the jar and close it up, continuing your manifestation mantra while you draw.

Express your gratitude by saying THANKS and expect the universe to manifest positive change in your life in the upcoming year!

~Week 7~
Building Friendships

◆◆◆

What You'll Need

Clay or Playdough (can be purchased or homemade)

Paper plate or tray

Preferable Location

Inside

Manifestation Exercise

Building friendships can be difficult, especially as adults. When we are out of school, if we don't have social situations set up to meet new people it can create a barrier to not only building friendships but to finding new friends. This exercise will help you to manifest new friends and create lasting friendships.

Take your clay and spread it out on your tray. Soften it so it is malleable. You are going to begin to mold it into a very specific shape, based on your desires and wants. Close your eyes and become one with the clay, feeling it in your hands, gently moving it into a cylindrical shape, stretching up and away from you. Now, imagine this is a tree trunk and you can feel it as it grows.

Next, begin, using your hands only, not your eyes, to pull branches out of the tree trunk, forming them naturally, gently and with love and care. Make as many branches as you'd like. Each branch will be different, as will each friendship, and will vary in length, again, as will each friendship. Say the words, 'I reach towards new friends,' as you continue pulling the branches with tenderness out of the trunk; you may find they overlap each other, or they curve around each other or they simply stick straight out and stay away from the other branches. However they form is ok, as each friendship will form it's own twists and turns and grow and change in time. As you pull each branch allow your conscious thought to be directed to manifesting and building friendships over the next year and be thankful!

~Week 8~
Drawing in Lasting Love

◆◆◆

What You'll Need

Multiple pieces of paper-preferably pink, red and white Pink candle (pink all the way through, glittery is perfect) Metal you can use to seal wax, pink ribbon

Preferable Location

Inside

Manifestation Exercise

There are many ways to draw in lasting love. This exercise will give you a chance to manifest someone who will be exactly what you're hoping for. Be sure you are in a safe place and be careful as you will be using the wax from your candle so have a fireproof plate under it before you begin. Then, light your candle.

Think about the attributes you are looking for in a mate-be specific. Think of hair color, eye color, height, body type, etc. But, take it further and think about the type of person you want. For example, do you want rustic, smart, adventurous, outgoing, well-read, musical, etc.? Focus next on how you want to feel when you are with your significant other to be. Tune into those feelings. Maybe there is excitement, happiness, contentedness, security and more. Continue imagining what traits you'd like in a partner.

Now, one at a time, write them down, one characteristic or feeling per paper. When you are all done writing each thing down, fold the pages, corners in, like an envelope. Then drip a drop of wax on the paper, sealing it with your metal object, while saying, 'I am manifesting my true love'. Do this with all of your traits and when you are done stack them together and tie the pink ribbon around them, repeating your mantra. Then, bring the bundle to your underwear drawer and tuck it underneath, in the back-left corner.

Give thanks for the love that's coming!

~Week 9~
Love Your Career

◆◆◆

What You'll Need

Red ribbon

Coins, warmed tumbled or soft stone

Preferable Location

Inside or outside

Manifestation Exercise

Loving your career means that you enjoy what you do. When you love what you do, you'll never have to work. This exercise will help you manifest this in your life, which will in turn help relieve and remove any stress you may have that's caused by a difficult work situation.

Take your red ribbon and wrap it gently, yet firmly, around your non-dominant hand, repeating the words, 'Within my hands I hold love for what I do.' Place the coins and the warmed stone in that hand. Carefully, using your mouth if necessary, wrap the same ribbon around your other hand. Then, wrap and join your two hands together, with the coins and the stone between them. As you wind the ribbon and pull your hands closer, continue to say the mantra above. When you've bound them, state with authority, 'Together, my hands create the power to love my career, now and forever.'

Your hands are an extension of you and your ribbon represents love. The coins are for financial freedom and the warm stone signifies grounding and warmth. Altogether, when joined, the entire exercise embodies loving your career. This exercise should be repeated every day over the next week to lock in your manifestation wish.

With each repetition, you may wish to add more objects to the coins and stone to represent the career you love. But, keep the exercise itself the same. Remember, give thanks for manifesting exactly what you need.

~Week 10~
Creating a Homelife You Love

◆◆◆

What You'll Need

Small box and ribbon to hold the following 5 objects:

Small heart-shaped object, gold colored coin, green leaf, your signature on a piece of paper, picture of happy family (yours or generic if you don't have one)

Preferable Location

Inside or outside

Manifestation Exercise

Creating a homelife you'll love involves covering all the basics-love, family, finances, career and health. You and only you are the one who knows what you want from each of these topics, and that makes you the perfect person to manifest the exact homelife you'll love. You'll address each aspect separately in order to pull it all together, allowing you to create a complete home.

Open your box. Hold your heart object in your hands and close your eyes. This represents love. Whether you are currently in a relationship or not, focus on what type of love you'd like to enjoy with a partner and say the words, 'I delight in nourishing love with my partner' 11 times, then place it in the box. Next, while holding your coin which represents finances, state, 'I have a constant and abundant financial inflow'. Now, it's time for family so pick up your picture and say 11 times, 'My family is happy and mutually supportive' before placing it with the other items in the box. Pick up your signature paper and imagine being in the perfect career, just for you, that makes you feel as though you're not even working and say out loud, 'I love what I do and get paid what I deserve', again, repeating 11 times before finally picking up your leaf. This represents your health. Hold this in your hand and 11 times pronounce, 'I am perfectly healthy', before adding it to your box.

Finally, tie the box with ribbon and place under your bed. Say THANK YOU to the universe for manifesting, for you, a wonderful homelife!

~Week 11~
Ability to Be Patient

◆◆◆

What You'll Need

Large pot of cold water

Stove or outdoor cooking fire

Preferable Location

Inside or outside

Manifestation Exercise

Finding patience can be trying in the best of times, but when you feel like time is flying by, as it usually seems to be, it is even more difficult. Patience, however, is an extremely important trait for all of us to possess, though it may often prove to be elusive. The following exercise will help you manifest patience across the board. Any time you feel your patience is waning in any area of your life you can do the exercise again and recharge your manifestation!

Place your pot of cold water on the heat, either on the stove inside or the cooking fire outside. Stay there until the water boils. This will take a bit of time. While you wait, meditate on a color rainbow, (red, orange, yellow, green, blue, indigo, violet) beginning at the base of your spine (red) moving up to the top of your head (violet). These are your chakras, or your energetic centers and they will help connect you to the universe and help you to manifest everything you need. Focus on each color individually, repeating it over and over, each time releasing your breath when you reach the top chakra (top of head) and breath out the word, 'Patience' aloud.

Continue doing this until the water boils, then remove the water from the heat, and reverse the process. Start from the top, closing down your chakras, breathing as you move down to the base of your spine, from violet down to red, breathing out the word, 'Patience' again when you reach the bottom each time, until the water cools down. When you are done, you might notice the pot of water has changed color. Dump it out slowly—you can even use it to water indoor or outdoor plants. Send gratitude to the universe for giving you the patience you need!

~Week 12~
Financial Abundance

◆◆◆

What You'll Need

12 Votive (or similar sized) candles,

a mix of gold and silver

Matches

Preferable Location

Inside

Manifestation Exercise

For this manifestation exercise you will need to be around for 12 hours so pick a day that'll work for this. You will also need to have somewhere safe to light allow the candles to burn without concern. As with all of your exercises, the belief that you are generating that which you desire is key to the manifestation of your wishes. Financial abundance is no different!

Place all 12 candles in a row, on candle safe holders, where they will not be disturbed or need to be moved. Light the first match and say, 'Lighting the first candle will ignite my financial abundance during this first month,' then light the first candle. Be sure it's burning and focus on the flame for a minute or two repeating the mantra. Then you may walk away.

Exactly one hour from the time you lit the first candle, return to light the second. If the first has gone out but can be relit, light it again and repeat the words. Then light the second candle, saying, 'Lighting the second candle will ignite my financial abundance during this second month.' Continue this over the next 12 hours, with each candle. Re-light each candle as needed and be sure to re-state any mantra connected to that particular candle if necessary.

When all of the candles have totally burned out and are done, nothing left to burn, bring them outside and bury the remains in the earth, saying, 'I plant the everlasting flame of financial abundance.'

Thank the universe for giving you the opportunity to experience financial abundance!

~Week 13~
Success in Career

◆◆◆

What You'll Need

Paper, scissors, pen, ribbon

Preferable Location

Outside

Manifestation Exercise

As with all of your manifesting, success in any area is really a personal thing. Your preferences are what matter because they are what make you happy. It is this assembly of inclinations that you will focus on to manifest a successful career. Beginning, of course, with what having a successful career means to you.

Go outside and cut your paper into strips you can write on. Now, on each strip, one at a time, write down what your successful career entails. Write down the type of career it is. Write down how it makes you happy. Write down your perfect hours and whether you'd work part time or full time. Write your ideal working location, whether it be from home or an office or at a specific location. Write on a strip who your boss(es) would be or if you are the boss. Write down any co-workers you'd like to have or employees or types of co-workers and employees. Write down what type of recognition you'd need to feel successful. Write down what your earning level would be in order to be successful in your career. Write down anything else you can imagine which would contribute to achieving your version of a successful career.

When you've finished take your ribbon and your strips and tie each statement to a tree, branch or bush. Spread them around, spreading your energy far and wide, while saying the words, 'I am successful in my career!' every time. Continue until you are totally done dispersing your wishes, knowing that you will manifest your career success!

Again, share your gratitude with the universe to send out your energy and appreciation!

~Week 14~
Peace Within

◆◆◆

What You'll Need

Clear quartz crystal

Preferable Location

Inside or Outside

Manifestation Exercise

In order to have peace within, sometimes it's necessary to remove anything that's not peaceful. This exercise can help you clear old energy and make room for new peaceful energy.

Go to a quiet place where you can focus only on you, without being disturbed. With your crystal in hand, bend to your feet and begin clearing out anything that holds us back from being at peace by saying, 'Allow any negativity to leave my spirit through this crystal.' Slowly, move the crystal up your body, from your toes to your ankles to your calves, etc., until you've reached all the way to the top of your head, repeating your clearing mantra as you go.

Now, you need to get rid of all of the energy you've injected into your crystal. Take it to the sink and rinse it with cold water. If you're outside, you'll need to find a stream or water to cleanse it or shake it until it feels lighter. As you hold the crystal under the water (or shake it) chant the words, 'Clear the negativity, make room for peace.' Continue until you feel ready to move to the next step.

Next, take the crystal, and the same way, starting from your toes, move it up your body, slowly. But, this time, you are charging your cleared energy with peaceful energy. As you move it up, this time chant the words, 'This crystal brings inner peace to my spirit,' over and over until you make it to the top of your head. Then hold the crystal against your heart and repeat the mantra again. Stay in this position until you feel a wave of peaceful energy spill down over you. You can re-do this exercise any time you feel you need a new dose of peace in your life, just rinse the crystal first. Be grateful you are able to manifest lasting inner peace!

~Week 15~
Peace Around You

◆◆◆

What You'll Need

Glitter

Preferable Location

Outside

Manifestation Exercise

There is a huge difference between inner peace and external peace. While manifesting peace in your spirit seems daunting enough, trying to create a peaceful environment can be even more difficult. That's why the magic of manifestation is so important; you can spread your energy all around, sending peace into the world.

Go outside. Take out your glitter. Begin by exclaiming, 'This glitter is peace external, and I spread it far and wide.' Now, gently, sift some glittery energy around you in a circle. Once you've done that, say the words again. Then, continue, wandering through the yard, the street, the town, allowing a bit of glitter to be released wherever you go. As you spread the glitter, continue chanting the words above.

Over the next week, increase your range. Go further and further out, extending past your town, even beyond your state if you're able. Spread the glitter and continue to chant the words. Continue broadening your peace as far as you're able, repeating your mantra, manifesting peace all around you, and then some.

Give thanks for the ability to spread peace and have it multiplied by everyone around you!

~Week 16~
Healing

◆◆◆

What You'll Need

Pink, light green and white ribbon

Preferable Location

Inside

Manifestation Exercise

Healing is a pretty broad word. It covers a wide spectrum of ailments. This exercise is designed to manifest an overall feeling of peace and healing. You can make it more specific for you depending upon your intention, but I suggest you focus on general healing first. Take the white ribbon and lay it out on the table. Lay your hands on it and say, 'My energy is clear to receive healing'. Repeat this three times, moving your hands over the entire white ribbon as you do. Next, take the pink ribbon and lay that to the right of the white ribbon, laying your hands on it and the white ribbon at the same time. State, 'I am filled with love and positive energy'. Repeat this five times, all the while continuing your contact with both the white and the pink ribbons. Lastly, lay the green ribbon down to the right of the pink one. Touch all three ribbons at the same time and focus your energy there. State aloud, 'I receive all positive healing energy.' Repeat this eight times while touching all of the ribbons.

Now, braid the ribbons together, and say, 'I allow healing.' When you are done, depending upon the length of the braid, you may wear it as a bracelet for the next week or a necklace, or simply put it in your pocket. Any time you feel as though you could use a dose of healing energy simply touch the ribbon braid and state, 'I manifest healing in all areas of my life.' To manifest more specific healing, simply insert what type you need by saying, 'I manifest _________ healing.'

Thank the universe for so easily and positively bestowing healing upon you!

~Week 17~
Being Comfortable Around Others

◆◆◆

What You'll Need

Comfortable socks and a warm snuggly blanket

Preferable Location

Inside

Manifestation Exercise

Before you can be comfortable around others you need to be comfortable yourself. For this exercise it's important you find somewhere you can hunker down and relax for a bit without being interrupted.

Put on your comfortable socks and notice how your feet feel. They should be cozy, snug and safe. This is how the rest of you needs to be in order to move forward. Next, it's time to wrap the blanket around you and feel how secure that makes you feel. Relish in the comfort that brings for a moment, while allowing yourself to feel relaxed and content.

Now, it's time to manifest that same feeling with others that you are experiencing alone. As you physically feel the blanket wrapped around you, keeping you safe and secure, say the following words out loud, 'I am as comfortable around others as I am with this blanket wrapped around me. When I am with others, I am wrapped in comfort and security.' Repeat this mantra 11 times, hugging the blanket around you.

Then, slowly remove the blanket and as you do say, 'I am comfortable wherever I am, especially around others,' and continue repeating this manifestation chant until you are completely unwrapped. When you are done, say it again, as you wiggle your toes in your comfortable socks.

Be grateful that the universe has your back and know that any time you need a dose of comfort you can re-wrap yourself in a blanket and repeat your manifestation mantra!

~Week 18~
Confidence

◆◆◆

What You'll Need

2 Crystals-Sunstone & Moonstone

Preferable Location

Outside

Manifestation Exercise

This exercise can be done with other crystals, such as rose quartz or even plain stones if you don't have access to these special rocks, but ideally, using Sunstone and Moonstone is the best way to access your confidence. Try and allow for 12 hours in between both parts of the exercise as you want to perform the manifestation in the morning and in the evening.

Bring your sunstone outside in the early morning, preferably when the sun is out. It can be a cold day, but the sun should be shining, not a rainy day. Sunstones help you to shine and helps to bring out hidden talents. So, holding your crystal up to the sun, eyes closed, say the words, 'I am powerful and confident and shine bright like the sun.' Repeat this 10 times as you slowly open your eyes, looking at your hands holding the crystal, sun in the background. Then, put your stone in your pocket and keep it there throughout the day, repeating your mantra anytime you find yourself touching it.

Once evening comes and the moon is in the sky go outside with your moonstone. This crystal can help to calm any fears or any phobias you may have so it can help to clear any unease that creates a lack of confidence, helping to dissipate any blocks to your manifestation. Hold your crystal up towards the moon and utter the words, 'I give the moon my angst leaving me with only confidence.' Repeat 11 times. Then place your moonstone in your pocket with your sunstone, allowing both energies to come together, bringing a balanced confidence to you.

Give thanks for the ability to manifest the confidence you need in your life!

~Week 19~
Projecting Kindness

◆◆◆

What You'll Need

Little sticky note papers, pen

Preferable Location

Outside

Manifestation Exercise

Projecting kindness seems like a funny thing to manifest but the reality is we all need to give ourselves a boost when it comes to sending kindness out to the universe. Manifesting kindness can simply begin as an act of compassion or humanity or even just a simple gesture towards someone else. Projecting kindness simply means we value others as well as ourselves and share positive energy that people can feel. A simple exercise in spreading this energy can get you well on your way to manifesting this kindness long term.

Take your sticky notes and pen and one at a time begin writing positive messages. Make them up--things you might like someone to say to you. Comments such as, 'You are nice!', 'You are kind!', 'You are worthy!', "You are beautiful!', 'You're amazing!', 'You are fantastic!', 'You're special!', 'You're brilliant!', etc. Continue writing these positive phrases on each sticky note saying each one aloud to yourself as you do.

When you've filled up all of your notes leave your home or where you are and go out into the world. Go to school or work or the mall or wherever you choose and begin leaving these sticky notes in places people will see them. In the bathroom, on a door, on a countertop, etc. Every time you place a note say the phrase out loud to yourself. When you are all done, say these words out loud, 'I project kindness to those around me now and always!' Repeat this every day for the next week.

Be thankful you have the opportunity to manifest kindness in your life with such ease!

~Week 20~
Creativity

◆◆◆

What You'll Need

Small envelope or box Colored paper Water

Preferable Location

Outside

Manifestation Exercise

Creativity comes in many ways and is different for many people. For this exercise you are going to work on manifesting what encompasses creativity overall, and what brings your creative energy to the surface.

Take all of your colored paper and slowly rip them into little bits and pieces. As you do, say the words, 'I manifest creativity in my life in every way.' Continue ripping all of the paper until it's torn so small that you can't physically make it any smaller. Then, put it all together, and mix it up. Say the words again, 'I manifest creativity in my life in every way.' As you mix the colors together, you are joining all of your creative energy together.

Now, sprinkle some of the water on the paper, joining it together, and smoosh it all up, shaping it into whatever form or design you want it to be, saying, 'I manifest creativity in my life in every way.' Then, add a few more sprinkles to your colored paper and reshape it, giving it new life and repeat your mantra. Do this three more times.

Finally, after you've created five different shapes, create a final shape that will fit into your envelope or box and, while placing the paper you've created into your container say the words, 'I am filled with an abundance of creative energy.'

Then, bring the entire package outside and bury it in the ground, repeating the mantra again, while expressing gratitude to the universe for the ability to manifest your creativity!

~Week 21~
Happiness

◆◆◆

What You'll Need

Music you like

Preferable Location

Inside or outside

Manifestation Exercise

Whenever I think of true happiness I think of Snoopy, the dog from Charlie Brown, who does the happy dance. To do the happy dance, you need music. So, for this exercise, you will play your favorite music. And, you will be alone, because this is to manifest YOUR happiness, no one else's. That's important. It is about you and that is who you need to focus on right now.

Turn on your music, and slowly turn it up. Stand up and begin moving around, sway back and forth, and start to dance. Feel the music. It doesn't matter if you think you can dance or not—just move. As you dance, smile. Smile through your body, all the way to the tips of your fingers and to the tips of your toes. And, dance.

As your dancing becomes stronger and your smile becomes wider let your spirit feel happiness flowing through it. Say the words, 'I am filled with overflowing happiness.' Keep dancing and let your smile get brighter, your dancing more powerful. Repeat your mantra. Enjoy the moment. It's just for you, this happiness that you are feeling, this pure joy, this feeling that there is nothing more but the dance of delight. Dance, and smile. Repeat your mantra.

You need do nothing else but enjoy the dance. State with conviction and total belief, 'I am filled with overflowing happiness.' Repeat as long as you choose to continue dancing, as long as it feels right to you.

Then, say thanks for the sheer joy you now have and will continue to experience.

~Week 22~
Stress Free Life

◆◆◆

What You'll Need

Paper, pen, fire place or fire pit or

somewhere to burn paper

Preferable Location

Inside or outside

Manifestation Exercise

For this exercise you are going to clear anything that causes you stress. Before you can lead a stress-free life, you have to remove the stressors from your life. This manifestation is simple, but very effective and can be used whenever something comes up throughout the year that causes you additional stress.

Begin by focusing on what is causing you stress. Get specific. For example, if it is finances, think of what it is about your financial situation that is stressing you out. Then write it down on a piece of paper. Tear that bit off from the rest of the paper. Then, focus on the next thing and write that down, and again, rip it away. Again, be sure to be very detailed. If you are vague about what is bothering you, it won't help you. The more definitive you are, the easier it will be to manifest the change in your life. Continue writing down everything that causes you stress until you've got all of the strips of paper in your hands.

Then, one by one, read them out loud and follow each one with the words, 'I release this stress forever,' and then throw it into the fire. After you've finished burning and releasing each stressor say, 'I am stress free!' Say this over and over until it feels right. Finally, extinguish the fire, cementing your manifestation.

Express your gratitude by thanking the universe for clearing the stress from your life from here on out!

~Week 23~
Will Power

◆◆◆

What You'll Need

Just yourself

Preferable Location

Inside or outside

Manifestation Exercise

Willpower is a difficult thing to possess. It's hard to overcome the obstacles that get in the way of whatever it is you are trying to accomplish when you are trying to use only willpower to accomplish it. Willpower usually only works as a temporary force, it is something that helps you get through things short-term. But, possessing will power, the ability to make it through these temporary situations will make it easier to make those transitory desires happen. This exercise will help you!

When you are ready, sit down and close your eyes. Relax. Think about your mind. You brain is composed of two different hemispheres. The right is in charge of creativity and imagination and intuition, whereas the left is in charge of logic and analytical thinking and numbers. Willpower has to overlap these two hemispheres in order to work and to be accessible for you. Think about how these two sections of your brain form your head and forehead area. Then relax for a moment, thinking about willpower and everything it can do for you.

Now, take your fingers, and gently but firmly and quickly begin tapping on your forehead while saying the words, 'I possess all the willpower I need to make all desired changes.' Continue stating the mantra aloud while crossing your hands and tapping the other side of your forehead, effectively crossing the hemisphere boundaries. Tap all the way around your crown area, continuing to cross and uncross as you go, repeating the words until you are ready to stop.

Then, thank the universe for assisting you in manifesting your ongoing willpower!

~Week 24~
Be Out In the World More

◆◆◆

What You'll Need

Thread, scissors

Preferable Location

Outside

Manifestation Exercise

Being out in the world more simply means putting yourself out there, even if it makes you feel uncomfortable. This can be difficult, especially when you are trying to break through any shyness or introvert tendencies you may have. This exercise will help you manifest the ability to overcome this by clearing safe pathways to get yourself more wanted exposure.

Go outside and bring your thread and scissors with you. This is your opportunity to create a path, send your energy into the world and manifest a more comfortable, more extroverted experience. So, begin by taking your thread in hand and throw it out into the yard, or the street, or the woods, holding onto the end. While you do, say the words, 'I am putting myself out in the world more, with ease.' Then cut the thread loose.

Move into a different location and do the same. Keep repeating the process, even going so far as to take your thread to an area that you want to actually expand into. For example, if you are hoping to publish a book, bring your thread to a bookstore, or a publishing house. Or, if it is new friendships to share new adventures with go to a place you'd like to hang out with friends and send your thread out while chanting the words, 'I am putting myself out in the world more, with ease.' Wherever you are, no matter the possible situation, visualize what you want to put into the world, and what outcome you're hoping for if you do, and send your thread out, repeating the mantra.

Express your gratitude by saying thanks to the universe for manifesting what you want!

~Week 25~
Creating Comfortable Space

◆◆◆

What You'll Need

Pillow

Preferable Location

Inside

Manifestation Exercise

Creating a comfortable space is about more than just buying stuff to fill a room. It's about a feeling and creating somewhere you can be that you feel good about yourself and others feel good when they join you.

This exercise is a simple one and can be done multiple times over the next week as the desire strikes you. Take your pillow and hug it close to your body. Feel the softness of it and how content it makes you feel. It can instantly calm you and make you feel at ease. Continue to hug this pillow and state the words, 'I am comfortable.'

Think of the different spaces in your life you'd like to make more comfortable for you and others and snuggle your pillow, repeating your mantra of, 'I am comfortable.' Then, think of any circumstances you wish to make more comfortable in your life and do the same.

Creating more comfortable space is as easy as manifesting comfort within yourself, so finally, hug your pillow and focus on how warm and fuzzy it makes you feel. Then, snuggle in with it a little more and repeat your words, 'I am comfortable.'

You are manifesting this one from the inside out. The more comfortable you are in your own skin, the more comfort you will create in the space around you. Be thankful you have the means to manifest this!

~Week 26~
Reliable Transportation

◆◆◆

What You'll Need

Piece of paper- about 2" x 4", pen

Preferable Location

Inside or outside

Manifestation Exercise

Reliable transportation can be interpreted in many ways. For this exercise we are going to focus on the ability to get to and from places easily, reliably, without worry.

Take your paper and pen to a table or somewhere you can draw on it. Imagine what a ticket would look like, a ticket you would have that would take you somewhere. It can look like a train ticket or a plane ticket or a bus ticket. It can look like a ticket you've never seen before. The important thing is that you are imagining it is a ticket that would provide you with reliable transportation.

Now, draw what you imagined on that ticket. Include any imagery and words you saw that you feel belong on the ticket for reliable transportation. As you draw, say the words, 'I always have reliable transportation,' repeatedly. Continue drawing your ticket. Include any additional images or words you can think of that relate to the type of transportation that you feel works for you. For instance, if it's reliable vehicle transportation you may want to draw images of a car or a truck or even write car or truck on the ticket. If it's taking a train on time or with convenience, draw a train or write the word train.

Continue repeating your mantra, 'I always have reliable transportation,' as you finish drawing your ticket. When you are done, imagine handing your ticket to a ticket collector who will guide you to your reliable transportation. And, one last time, repeat your mantra.

Then, give thanks for manifesting your wishes!

~Week 27~
Healthy Sex Life

◆◆◆

What You'll Need

Red & pink candles

Preferable Location

Inside or outside

Manifestation Exercise

For this exercise your focus will be on manifesting a fun, healthy, frequent sex life. This is not specifically about a new relationship or even an old relationship. It's about having great sex, regardless of where you are at in a relationship.

Bring your candles and a fire safe plate somewhere you won't be disturbed. Hold the candles in your hands, unlit. Feel the smoothness of the wax and notice how soft they are. Stay with them for a moment as you imagine the type of healthy sex life you'd like to have.

Now, light the candles. Slowly, as the candles begin to burn, pour the wax, one candle at a time, without extinguishing the flame, into the fire safe plate, blending the wax from the candles together. As you do, say following aloud, 'I enjoy a healthy sex life.'

Continue blending the wax of the candles together, while stating your mantra out loud. You can even take a spoon or a fork and stir the wax, blending it together as you would blend your energies together with someone to have healthy sex.

Allow the candles to continue to burn, mingling the wax, repeating the mantra over and over again until you are content or until the candles are depleted. When you are finished, if you're able, bring the wax outside and plant it in soil, reiterating again, 'I enjoy a healthy sex life.'

Thank the universe for allowing you the opportunity to have a wonderful, sexy life!

~Week 28~
Time to Enjoy Life

◆◆◆

What You'll Need

Bubbles

Preferable Location

Outside

Manifestation Exercise

This exercise is designed to manifest the time you need to enjoy life. So often we find time flying by, without enough hours in the day to accomplish what we need to and still have enough moments left to enjoy life.

Bring your container of bubbles outside. Begin by blowing bubbles into the air, counting each one as they float away. Keep sending the bubbles out, counting them as you do. When you get to your 100th bubble, say the words, 'I now have time to enjoy life.'

Resume your bubble blowing until you get to your 200th bubble and repeat the mantra. Continue all the way up to 1,000 bubbles, re-stating your mantra in increments of 100. Watch the bubbles as they float, shimmering and iridescent. Look at all of the colors they reveal. Count how many different shades you see as they drift away.

Then, repeat your mantra, 'I now have time to enjoy life.' Thank the universe for manifesting all the time you need to enjoy your life!

~Week 29~
Relaxation

◆◆◆

What You'll Need

Just yourself

Preferable Location

Inside or outside

Manifestation Exercise

Relaxation seems like such a simple concept, but in the world we live in it can be a most difficult undertaking. Achieving relaxation is a necessity not only for enjoying life, but for our health as well. Manifesting relaxation should be something that you will continue to work on for the rest of your life, but this exercise will jumpstart you.

Go somewhere you won't be interrupted for the next 10 minutes and where you can sit quietly. You will need to be comfortable, so try and wear comfortable clothing, or pants you can unbutton if necessary.

When you are situated, and ready, sit with your arms rested, hold your hands calmly in front of you, middle finger gently touching your thumb, and breathe. Take a deep breath in and release your breath. On the next breath in, think the words, 'I manifest complete relaxation.' As you exhale, release everything but relaxation.

Continue breathing and repeating your mantra. With every breath relax deeper and deeper, manifesting now by saying the words after every breath. When you feel completely relaxed you are done, though you can repeat this every day, all week long, if it feels right.

Express your gratitude by thanking the universe for not only allowing you to experience relaxation but promoting relaxation in your life.

~Week 30~
Enjoying Exercise

◆◆◆

What You'll Need

Nothing

Preferable Location

Inside or outside

Manifestation Exercise

For this exercise you'll need to be ready to move, so whether you are inside or outside doesn't matter. You simply need to be somewhere you can spread out.

Spread your hands out wide to your sides and point your face up towards the ceiling or the sky. As you do, say the words, 'I feel amazing!' Next, begin turn ing clockwise, in the same manner, saying the words, 'Movement makes me happy!' Continue, turning clockwise, slowly as to not make yourself dizzy, and repeat your mantra.

Now, add laughter. As you look up with your hands stretched out palms reaching up, say the words, 'I feel great when I exercise!' Repeat it again. Continue your mantra and your spinning. Do this 21 times, turning and saying it aloud. When you are done, put down your hands and feel how your body feels now. Say the words, 'I enjoy exercising' 12 times.

The following day, repeat the entire manifestation exercise, adding a twist at your waist. After your spins, twist 21 times, and restate all of the mantras together, 'Movement makes me happy! I feel great when I exercise! I enjoy exercising!'

The day after that, add a toe touch, and do the same as above. Repeat this all week, restating the entire mantra after your spins, twists and toe touches.

Thank the universe for helping you to manifest the ability to enjoy and even desire exercise!

~Week 31~
Travel

◆◆◆

What You'll Need

Map

Preferable Location

Inside or outside

Manifestation Exercise

This exercise can be done with a designation in mind or without. You can tailor it to meet your needs.

Take your map out. Close your eyes and place your hands gently on the map. Begin moving them around. As you move them, visualize your feet on ground they've never walked upon, or perhaps somewhere they've been, but where you want to travel again.

Continue moving your hands lightly over the map and say the words, 'I welcome travel into my life.' If the travel you want is for pleasure, than use the mantra, 'I welcome travel for pleasure into my life.' If it is for work, change it to, 'I welcome travel for work into my life.' But, if you wish to travel for all reasons, just leave it without specifying. For example, if you are an author, and want to travel for book events and have fun while doing it simply say 'I welcome travel into my life.'

If you want to travel worldwide, be sure to use a map that covers the areas you want to visit. If you want to travel only domestically, use local maps only. Continue with your mantra, visualizing your feet on land you wish to travel to, whether you know where you're going or not.

Repeat your mantra, until it feels as though your spirit has actually traveled. Then open your eyes and see where your hands are. Notice if it is somewhere you want to go or if it's somewhere you want to be. If not, that's ok--it represents travel everywhere.

Thank the universe for finding your next destination and for bringing travel into your life!

~Week 32~
Having Fun

◆◆◆

What You'll Need

A small ball

Preferable Location

Outside

Manifestation Exercise

For this exercise you need to be prepared to move around. Go somewhere you will have space.

Take the small ball in your hand. Begin tossing it in the air with one hand and catching it with the other hand. Then, start turning around as you continue tossing the ball. If you drop it, it's ok, keep going. Now, go faster. Spin. Toss the ball. You will drop the ball. You will laugh. This is good!

Keep going. As you do, say the words, 'I bring fun into my life, enjoying every moment!' Spin faster, laugh harder and throw the ball higher. Enjoy the moment. Repeat the mantra. It may even begin to feel a bit manic as you echo your mantra, over and over again.

Keep up the fun; continue spinning, throwing and laughing. Restate your mantra, 'I bring fun into my life, enjoying every moment!' Continue until you are laughing so much you need to stop, or you feel like you will collapse on the ground in laughter. Then, do sit or lay down on the ground. Look to the sky. Hold your ball up. Repeat your manifestation, 'I bring fun into my life, enjoying every moment!'

Do this every day for the next week. If necessary, do it inside, just be mindful when you are tossing the ball that you don't break anything.

Be grateful that you will have fun throughout the rest of the year!

~Week 33~
Spending More Time With Your Kids

◆◆◆

What You'll Need

Pictures of your children, white candles

to match number of kids

Twine and scissors to cut it

Preferable Location

Inside

Manifestation Exercise

This exercise is meant to bring you together with your kids in a healthy, happy way.

When you are ready, wrap a piece of twine around the first candle. Then, roll up the first picture, binding it with a second piece of twine cut from the end of the same twine you used to wrap the candle. Then, place the picture in front of the candle. Repeat the process with each candle, matching it to one of your children's pictures.

When you are done with each of your kids, it's time to light the candles, one at a time. As you do, say the words, 'With this flame, I happily ignite the time spent with ______.' (Insert their name.) Repeat this with each candle for your kids. Reiterate your mantra three times, going through each person. When you have finished, allow the candles to continue to burn for a minimum of 15 minutes. Repeat your manifestation phrase.

Now, unwrap each picture, one by one, beginning with the child you started with, and say the words, 'I open __________ up to spending positive time together with me.' (Again, insert your child's name.) Do this for each of your kids and restate it three times.

Let the candles burn for another 15 minutes. When you are done, blow out the candles. Then, wrap together the pictures of your children, giving thanks for the time you will spend together!

~Week 34~
A Successful Renovation

◆◆◆

What You'll Need

4 Nails & string

Preferable Location

Outside

Manifestation Exercise

This exercise is meant to bring about a successful renovation project. This can be used when you already have plans in the works or before you've begun the undertaking.

Bring your nails and your string outside. Take the nails and place one at each corner of the entire building you are renovating, regardless of how much of the structure you are actually renovating. As you place each nail on the ground, repeat the words, 'With this nail I circle my renovation with success!'

After you've placed each nail, go back and pick them up, one by one. When you've collected them all take your string and bind them all together, wrapping the string up and down the nails, covering them. Then, say the words 'With these nails, I bind my renovation with success!'

Now, bring the bound nails somewhere on the property, preferably near the place you are renovating, and bury them in the earth. As you bury them, state the words, 'With these nails, I manifest a successful renovation!'

When you've finished burying them, say the words, 'The renovation is grounded in success!' Repeat this 21 times.

Express your gratitude by thanking the universe for manifesting a successful renovation.

~Week 35~
Intuition

◆◆◆

What You'll Need

Glass of water, quartz or amethyst crystal

Preferable Location

Inside or outside

Manifestation Exercise

You will be using water for this exercise, so be sure you are somewhere that you won't mind getting wet. Wear clothing that can get wet as well.

Dip your crystal into the water. Then, take the wet crystal and rub it across your forehead and say the words, 'My intuition is growing stronger every day.' Do this 21 times. Allow the water to drip down your face as you do, making the manifestation spread stronger throughout your psychic self.

Dip the crystal back into the water. Drip it over the very top of your head and repeat your manifestation, 'My intuition is growing stronger every day.' Again, do this 21 times, allowing the crystal to transfer it's energy through the water.

Repeat the process three more times, restating your manifestation mantra each time. When you are done, pour the remaining water over your head, stating, 'My intuition is growing stronger every day.' Allow the water to travel down over you as you continue asserting your mantra aloud.

When it feels as though the water is no longer trickling, declare your manifestation one more time. Then, thank the universe for helping you tune into your intuition more than ever before!

~Week 36~
Change

◆◆◆

What You'll Need

Bowl of 12 ice cubes, empty mug and hot water

Preferable Location

Inside or outside

Manifestation Exercise

You can use this exercise for changing any number of things in your life. It can be used for overall change or something more specific. Most importantly, it should be used for positive change. Remember, change usually doesn't happen instantly, but by beginning the process you are bringing about the manifestation of change.

You'll need a bit of time, so be sure to do this when you won't be disturbed. Begin your manifestation—take out one ice cube and place it in the mug. State aloud, 'I am currently _____.' (Fill in the blank with something you'd like to change.) Then, take the hot water and pour it over the ice while saying, 'I am changing it to __________.' Continue stating this until the ice has fully melted.

Once you've done the first ice cube, repeat with the remaining 11 cubes. You may continue to use the same issue you'd like to change or make additional statements for other things you'd like to change.

Once you've finished, state aloud, 'I welcome positive change in every way.' Then, be thankful you're able to manifest change for your greater good!

~Week 37~
Stepping Into Your Power

◆◆◆

What You'll Need

3 Different types of shoes (i.e. exercise, work, play)

Preferable Location

Outside

Manifestation Exercise

Be prepared to walk a little for this manifestation. If you are unable to actually walk you can go through the motions by moving your shoes.

Put on your first set of shoes and walk. As you begin to walk say aloud with each pace, 'I am stepping into my power with each stride.' Walk for at least seven minutes, continuing to say your manifestation mantra. You can walk as quickly or as slowly as you'd like, as long as you don't stop reiterating your statement.

Once you've finished, change shoes. Do the same thing in your new pair. Again, you can determine your own pace, it won't change how slowly or quickly you are able to manifest stepping into your own power. But, do not stop repeating your mantra, 'I am stepping into my power with each stride.'

Finally, switch into your last pair of shoes. Walk for at least seven minutes chanting your mantra repeatedly the entire time. When you've finished, take off your shoes and wiggle your toes. Then, place your feet on the ground. Take seven steps and say, 'I step into my power.'

Thank the universe for helping you to manifest your power!

~Week 38~
Reaching A Goal

◆◆◆

What You'll Need

Paper, pen, small box

Preferable Location

Inside or outside

Manifestation Exercise

This is a manifestation to be able to reach your goal. You can then use it to reach a specific goal you create. Then, you can use it to help you attain other goals you set for yourself.

Take out your pen and paper. Write down the goal you wish to reach in sentence form. Once you've done that, take the sentence and draw the words out into an image. Focus on the image and say the words, 'I will __________.' (Insert your goal here.)

Repeat this mantra 21 times while retracing the image you've created. Once you're done, take the paper and fold it up as small as you possibly can, reiterating your manifestation. Then, place it inside the box. Put the box under your bed, and state your mantra again, 'I will __________.'

Then, let it go. Thank the universe for manifesting your goal. Allow it to happen and leave your box alone. If you want to manifest another goal, you can add it to your box, but do not unfold your previous papers.

~Week 39~
Strength

◆◆◆

What You'll Need

Piece of wood (about 12 inches long), twine

Preferable Location

Inside or outside

Manifestation Exercise

Strength is something that comes from deep within. We all can use a little help mustering up the strength we need to accomplish something, or to just get through the daily troubles we face in life. This exercise will help you manifest the ability to pull up the strength you require.

Take your piece of wood and begin wrapping the twine around it. As you do, repeat the words, 'I am strong, as strong as wood.' Continue wrapping the twine around it, making even the wood stronger as you manifest your own strength.

Keep wrapping the twine around the wood until the wood is completely covered. Once you're done, say the words, 'I am strong down deep, and use my strength to accomplish everything I need to.' Keep the wood accessible so you can take it out anytime you need to muster up any additional strength.

Thank the universe for manifesting great spiritual, emotional and physical strength for you!

~Week 40~
Spending More Time With Friends

◆◆◆

What You'll Need

Paper, scissors, watch or clock

Preferable Location

Inside

Manifestation Exercise

Spending more time with friends doesn't mean neglecting your responsibilities or ignoring what you need to do. It simply means you get the opportunity to spend more quality time together with people who are important to you.

Take your paper and cut out shapes of people with your scissors, like paper dolls. Cut out as many as you want. It's not about the quantity, it's what they represent. If there are specific people you'd like to spend more time with you can even write their names on the cutouts.

Now, one by one, take your paper people and place them on your timepiece. As you do, say the words, 'Time extends as my friendships expand.' Continue stating this phrase with each paper friend until you're done.

Then, state aloud, 'I have plenty of time to enjoy my friendships on a regular basis.' Say this 11 times while holding your paper friends and your clock. When you are done, leave them together for the next week, and repeat your mantra three times a day. Then, put your paper in your closet under your clothes and put the clock away.

Express your gratitude to the universe by saying thanks for manifesting more quality time together with friends.

~Week 41~
Pure Joy

◆◆◆

What You'll Need

Glitter, white & pink candles

Preferable Location

Inside or outside

Manifestation Exercise

There is so much to be joyful about! Sometimes, however, we need a little help to experience that joy. This exercise will help you manifest it.

Bring your candles and your glitter somewhere that makes you happy. Light each candle and allow the smoke of the candles to rise up. Then, sprinkle the glitter onto the candles, allowing the glitter to mesh with the wax and blend. You may even see pops of color as it touches the flame.

As you do this, state, 'I find joy in everything!' Repeat this as you continue to sprinkle the glitter over the candles. Say it aloud at least 21 times, by the third time be sure to add a smile to your face.

Watch how fun and interesting it is as the glitter touches down on the candles and by the tenth time saying your mantra begin laughing out loud.

When you have repeated, 'I find joy in everything!' at least 21 times pour the rest of the glitter slowly on the candles, careful not to catch anything on fire. Then, allow the candles to keep burning, extinguishing naturally.

Be thankful for the joy you are experiencing now and the abundant joy you are manifesting for your future!

~Week 42~
New Home

◆◆◆

What You'll Need

Magazine pictures of houses or printouts of houses

Preferable Location

Inside or outside

Manifestation Exercise

This manifestation is a simple one to welcome in a new home that you will enjoy and be comfortable in.

Look at all of the pictures you have and focus on the features you'd like to have or that you appreciate in a new home. Once you've gone through all of the pictures, say these words aloud, 'Floors, windows, ceilings and walls, a new home is where my heart is called.'

Continue repeating these words 21 times. Then, visualize what you want in a home. Imagine the size, the color, the number of floors, bedrooms and bathrooms and the basic style of the house. Visualize any other specifics or details you are looking for in a new home.

Now, with your desires for your new home in your mind, say the words, 'I manifest a perfect new home for me!' Repeat that 21 times while visualizing what you want.

When you are done, put your pictures in a special place and let it go. Be grateful your wishes for a new home will be manifested!

~Week 43~
New Car

◆◆◆

What You'll Need

Small piece of rubber, small piece of metal, small bag

Preferable Location

Inside or outside

Manifestation Exercise

What an exciting time! You are thinking about getting a new car! Instead of merely thinking about it, manifest it and make it happen!

Begin thinking about what type of car you'd like to have. Do you want a sports car? An SUV? A truck? A 2-door or 4-door? What color do you want? All wheel drive? Front wheel drive? Standard or automatic? Get specific about what you are looking for. Now, take your rubber and metal pieces and put them together into a bag. Shake the bag and visualize the rubber and metal becoming your fabulous new car. Keep shaking and say the words, 'Rubber and metal become one, bring me a car for work and fun.' Repeat this 11 times while shaking your bag and visualizing your new vehicle.

When you are done you can bring your 'new car bag' to a place where you will park your new car and leave it there. Either hang it in the space somehow or place it in the corner or the side of the parking space. You decide where to put it but leave it where it makes the most sense to you. Repeat your manifestation again, 'Rubber and metal become one, bring me a car for work and fun.'

Be grateful for the new car that is to come!

~Week 44~
New Abilities

◆◆◆

What You'll Need

Small bag, Bunch of different colored stones or crystals

Preferable Location

Inside or outside

Manifestation Exercise

This exercise is meant to be used to manifest new abilities of any type, in any field. Whether you wish to develop new intuitive abilities or musical abilities or educational abilities doesn't matter. This manifestation will bring about the conduit to allow these gifts to open up to you. This will be best accomplished at dawn or as close to sunrise as possible.

Decide if you want to focus on one new gift or if you'd like to welcome in many different abilities. If it's only one you want to concentrate on, all of your rocks will be for that one skill. If you want to direct your energy to multiple abilities, decide which stone or crystal you feel connected to for each one you'd like to attain.

Take out your first stone. Think about what new ability you'd like to have—it can be a new psychic ability or a new talent or even the capacity to better handle tough situations. Whatever you desire, focus on that as you hold the stone in your hands. Then, say the words, 'I have confidence in my abilities, the future is ripe with possibilities.' Repeat this 11 times then put the stone in your bag.

Hold the next stone in your hands. If you mean to manifest only one new ability, focus on the same one again. Or, focus on the new ability you've assigned to this particular stone if you want to obtain multiple gifts. Reiterate the mantra 11 times and put it in the bag. Then, repeat with each stone.

When you are all done, close the bag and be thankful your new abilities are on their way!

~Week 45~
New Job

◆◆◆

What You'll Need

Paper & 2 different colored markers

Preferable Location

Inside or outside

Manifestation Exercise

You can do this manifestation exercise outdoors if you want to specifically get a job working outside. Otherwise, it will be easier to do it inside. Assign one of the colored markers to skills you have, and one to what you'd like to do.

In the center of your paper, write your name with both markers; you can overlap the letters. Then, with the first marker, all around the paper, write down the large variety of skills you have. The skills you list can be anything from riding a skateboard to writing poetry to saving someone's life. After each one, draw a circle around the words and a line from the circle leading back to your name. When you are done, read all of your skills aloud.

Now, with the other marker, around the outside, write down all of the different things you would like to have in a new job. Put on your paper what type of business you'd like to work for, what type of responsibilities you want and how much money you'd want to make. Write down anything else you can think of that describes your dream job. When you've finished, draw squares around each thing and draw a line from each square to your name. Then, read each of your desires about your new job out loud.

Finally, say the words, 'My new job is on its way to me, I will enjoy it and it will be.' Repeat this 11 times.

Express your appreciation by thanking the universe for manifesting the best job for you!

~Week 46~
Inclusion by Others Socially

◆◆◆

What You'll Need

11 Stick matches, red marker, string

Preferable Location

Inside or outside

Manifestation Exercise

Inclusion by others socially is an interesting concept and one that can be difficult to achieve. Manifesting this will help it actually come to fruition.

Take one match stick and color the entire thing red with your marker. This match represents you. Say the words, 'I am whole by myself.'

Once you've finished, take all of the other matches and place them around your match, encircling it from all sides. Then, take your string and wrap it around the matches and tie it, creating a tight bundle. Now, say the words, 'I am whole by myself and happy and content when surrounded by others.'

Bring your bundle somewhere you can safely light it on fire. When you are ready set it to flame, saying aloud, 'We are united and ignited by our interests and individuality.' Continue repeating this mantra while you watch the grouping of matches burn until there is nothing left.

Accept that the universe is now working to bring people into your life who are for your greater good. These people will be welcoming and warm and will include you and support you in social settings. Be thankful the universe is manifesting this on your behalf!

~Week 47~
Balance

◆◆◆

What You'll Need

Round jar, flat piece of wood or ruler, bunch of pennies

Preferable Location

Inside or outside

Manifestation Exercise

This exercise is meant to be symbolic to represent the balance in your life. It will balance your external self with your internal self. If you are hoping to manifest balance between two specific elements in your life you can substitute them instead.

Take out your round jar and lay it flat on its side. Then take your piece of wood and balance it over the jar. Now, take one penny and place it on the left side of the wood—let it represent one part of your external self you wish to achieve balance in. This can be your work, your family, your socialization or fun times, your friends, etc.

Next, take another penny and place it on the other side, representing your internal self—your health, your love, your spirit, your mind, and more. Continue balancing your pennies, and your life, until the wood is level and no longer tips to one side or the other. Say the words, 'I am balanced in all areas of my life,' 11 times, being sure your pennies remain even.

If there is something you wish to achieve balance in now is the time to imagine each side represents what you need to equalize and add more pennies respectively. Repeat your mantra, 'I am balanced in all areas of my life,' but add the words, 'specifically with ________________' (add what you are trying to balance here). Say this 11 times.

When you are done remove the pennies and wash them under cold water. Then, put them in your pocket, restating your manifestation 3 times. Add a big Thank You to the universe when you are done!

~Week 48~
Connections to Others

◆◆◆

What You'll Need

Bottle of liquid bubbles

Preferable Location

Outside

Manifestation Exercise

For this exercise you may want to enlist the help of someone else who can drive you around in a car. Otherwise, only perform it when you are stopped somewhere.

Begin by going outside and blow some bubbles high into the air. As you watch the bubbles float away say the words, 'The bubbles reach to touch the world.' Now, go somewhere else. Get in a car and drive to a busy parking lot of the mall or a grocery store or another busy location.

Then, blow the bubbles up into the air, repeating your manifestation mantra. Move around the lot or the store and continue blowing the bubbles into the air saying your phrase again. Then, go to another busy location.

If you have someone driving you, lean out the window (safely) and blow your bubbles as you go, through traffic, as you pass people on the street. Be sure to also say your mantra to yourself and aloud as you do.

Go to as many different crowded locations you can until you run out of bubble liquid. When you are totally finished blowing bubbles and repeating your mantra, state aloud, 'I have sent myself out into the world, connecting to many new people.'

Be grateful for all of the help the universe is giving you to manifest your connections to others!

~Week 49~
Athleticism

◆◆◆

What You'll Need

Sneakers

Preferable Location

Inside or outside

Manifestation Exercise

Use this exercise to increase your athletic prowess overall. As usual, you can adapt it if you want to focus on one specific athletic skill. Take your sneakers and begin putting them on. As you slip your right foot into the first one, imagine you are like a superhero, donning the equivalent of a cape. Say the phrase, 'I am stepping into my athleticism.' Then, do the same with your left foot.

Now, moving back to your right sneaker, begin tying your laces, saying the words, 'These laces cross boundaries and bring together my ability and dexterity in all things sporty.' Again, repeat with your left foot.

Then, stand up and lift your right foot up, stating, 'With every step I become more agile and physical.' Do it again with your left foot. Turn around in a circle and declare, 'I am actively increasing my athleticism.'

Finally, bend over and touch your feet, your superhero costume, and state, 'I am strong, powerful and highly athletic.' Restate this mantra 12 times. Do this every day for the entire week to come.

Thank the universe for helping you manifest your athleticism!

~Week 50~
Quicker Thinking

◆◆◆

What You'll Need

Nothing

Preferable Location

Inside or outside

Manifestation Exercise

This exercise is very simple, even though you're using your brain. There are no special tools you need, only your own hands.

Begin by taking your hands and massaging the top of your head. Then, rub the back and the sides of your head. As you do, imagine your brain opening. Massage some more, imagining your cerebrum, the thinking part of your brain, expanding and growing. Rub your head even more and feel your brain, your cerebrum, pulsing, ready at a second's notice, to process thought.

Now, using your nails, gently scratch the top, sides and back of your head. Imagine there is an electric current traveling through your head, from your fingertips, sparking and igniting your brain to rapidly process all of your thoughts.

Continue with a mix of massage and scratching and state this phrase aloud, '1, 2, 3, 4, 5, with every thought I have I come alive.' Repeat this over and over again while you maintain your hand movements. Visualize the increasingly pulsing cerebrum while the electricity flows and opens your mind.

Finally, while continuing to state your mantra, move your hands over your head, your ears, your eyes and your mouth. Do this 11 times, stimulating your main sensory input areas.

Be grateful the universe has provided you with a mind that can be trained to respond and think quickly!

~Week 51~
Money Now

◆◆◆

What You'll Need

Paper and pen

Preferable Location

Inside and/or outside

Manifestation Exercise

This exercise is not for long term cash flow. It is for a specific amount of money that is needed immediately, right now.

The first part of this manifestation exercise requires homing in on the specific dollar amount that you desire right now. It is crucial to be explicit for this to work. So, the first thing you need to do is really think about how much money you need. Focus on the reason you feel you need the money and add up any expenses or bills you have that you need the money for so you can get a true total for what is necessary immediately.

Grab your paper and pen and write down the dollar amount you need in big giant numbers in the center of the page.

Then, around the outside, write down the reason(s) you need it. For example, if it is to pay your mortgage or your rent, write that down and include the total. If it is to pay a car payment, list that and the dollar amount. Keep writing everything down until you've finished recording what is essential for you to have now. Then, imagine what that money looks like. Visualize it in your hands. Pay attention to how it feels; the weight and the texture. Count it in your hands to make sure it is exactly what you want. Finally, say the words, 'In my hand soon will be $_________ (insert your amount) just for me.' 21 times. Repeat this hourly until the money manifests for you!

Be thankful for what you have now, what you've had before and what you'll have soon!

~Week 52~
More Laughter In Life

◆◆◆

What You'll Need

Just yourself

Preferable Location

Inside and outside

Manifestation Exercise

Be ready to laugh! This is a hands-on exercise, one that you will fully participate in—loudly!

To create more laughter in laugh you need to begin by laughing. So, with that said, place your hands on your belly and start with a light chuckle. Laugh out loud and notice how it feels in your belly. You may find you are laughing but your mouth isn't moving. Do it again. This time make sure you smile as you chuckle. Notice how it feels different in your body. You might even discover your smile stays on your face even after you've stopped laughing.

Now, really laugh. Allow yourself to have a full belly laugh, hands on your stomach area, mouth smiling wide. Let it last a full 15 seconds. When you are done, say the words, 'My laughter is happy and contagious, it is never angry or outrageous!' And then, laugh again, for 30 whole seconds, repeating your mantra when you are done.

It's time to take it a step further. Go outside and laugh. Then, go to the store or a public venue and laugh. Re-iterate your mantra again, often, to yourself as you're laughing. Go for the full, deep, down to your core laughter. This is the kind of laugh that makes you feel good no matter how you were feeling.

You are bringing laughter into your laugh by sending it out into the universe. Continue your laughter and repeat your manifestation mantra in any place you frequent, and everywhere you want to manifest more laughter. Your life will welcome it! Have gratitude for your joy!

WRAPPING IT UP

Now that you've discovered how easy it is to manifest what you want, and what you need, you may have also discovered that not everything happened the way you thought it would. In some instances, there's a good possibility you received what you asked for and didn't even realize it. Think about things that have happened or changes in your life and where they may relate in your manifestation process. You might be surprised!

If you let go of limiting beliefs there is a much greater probability your manifestations will come to fruition. You receive what you want as long as it's for your greater good. If you didn't manifest what you were hoping for there may be a reason. For example, perhaps now is not the right time for a career change because you needed to use your current health insurance for something unforeseen. Or maybe you didn't move because the perfect house wasn't available to you, yet. But, stay positive. You can run any of the specific manifestation exercises again. Believe you deserve to receive and your mind will help you achieve it! You've no doubt manifested many new realities into your life throughout this book, but the most important of all is your happiness—enjoy!!

∞

Other titles & products by Melanie Barnum

∞

Interpreting Intuitive Messages
The Book of Psychic Symbols
Melanie Barnum

PSYCHIC
DEVELOPMENT
BEYOND BEGINNERS
Develop a Deeper Understanding of Your Intuition
MELANIE BARNUM

LLEWELLYN'S
Little Book of
PSYCHIC
DEVELOPMENT
MELANIE BARNUM

Psychic
Abilities
For Beginners
Awaken Your Intuitive Senses
Melanie Barnum

MELANIE BARNUM
PSYCHIC
VISION
DEVELOPING YOUR CLAIRVOYANT
AND REMOTE VIEWING SKILLS

"An amazing book that gives enlightened awareness of the greatness within you. If you're ready to change your life *The Steady Way to Greatness* is a must read."
—Melissa Alvarez, author of *365 Ways to Raise Your Frequency*

The *Steady* Way to *Greatness*

Liberate Your Intuitive Potential & Manifest Your Heartfelt Desires

MELANIE BARNUM

Psychic Symbols
Oracle Cards
Receive, Interpret & Understand
Psychic Messages
A 45 - Card Deck
Melanie Barnum

Made in the USA
Middletown, DE
26 August 2019